Fronteras Americanas

Also by Guillermo Verdecchia

The Adventures of Ali & Ali and the aXes of Evil
   (with Marcus Youssef and Camyar Chai)*
Another Country / bloom*
Citizen Suárez*
Insomnia (with Daniel Brooks)
A Line in the Sand (with Marcus Youssef)*
The Noam Chomsky Lectures (with Daniel Brooks)*
The Terrible But Incomplete Journals of John D.

*Available from Talonbooks

Fronteras Americanas
(American Borders)

Second Edition
GUILLERMO VERDECCHIA

TALONBOOKS

Talonbooks
278 East First Avenue, Vancouver, British Columbia, Canada V5T 1A6
www.talonbooks.com

Third printing, second edition: October 2018

Typeset in Adobe Garamond and Frutiger
Printed and bound in Canada on 100% post-consumer recycled paper

Cover design by Christopher Wadsworth / Reactor

Talonbooks gratefully acknowledges the financial support of the Canada Council for the Arts, the Government of Canada through the Canada Book Fund, and the Province of British Columbia through the British Columbia Arts Council and the Book Publishing Tax Credit.

Library and Archives Canada Cataloguing in Publication
Verdecchia, Guillermo
        Fronteras Americanas : (American borders) / Guillermo Verdecchia. — 2nd ed.
A play.
Includes bibliographical references.
Also issued in electronic format.
Text in English.
ISBN 978-0-88922-705-7
        I. Title.
PS8593.E67F7 2012   C812'.54   C2012-904903-4

Para mis padres, Elvira y Rafael
and, this time, for my kids, Anaïs and Theo, también

Contents

Foreword

When my family came to Canada, the designation for us was displaced persons, usually shortened to DPs and often alliteratively decorated with "dirty." Other decades have produced their own formulations of national otherness: immigrants and foreigners, refugees and aliens, newcomers and new Canadians. Terminology apart, these people's journeys are all different and all the same. *Fronteras Americanas* is a vivid and arresting theatre piece drawn from its creator's own singular migration. But Guillermo Verdecchia both de-constructs and re-constructs the model in his personal meditation on displacement, and indeed, in his celebration of it.

Guillermo Verdecchia's own origins are Latin, and his agenda here is the investigation of the Latino stereotypes and received notions that get in the way of true perception. The playwright's dossier overflows with devastating data from pop culture, tourist guides, lifestyle journalism, commercials, advertising, and supermarket shelves. Historical briefings and quizzes and lectures – both mock and unmoving-eyeball serious – share the platform with audio and visual samples. He annotates furiously, flicking political, historical, linguistic, musical, moral, sexual, even Terpsichorean challenges at us as we scramble to gain a foothold in his demanding new topography. His range of references is vast and truly pan-American: Federico García Lorca and Ricky Ricardo, made-for-TV drug-cartel movies and Carlos Fuentes, the Zoot Suit Riots and *Chico and the Man*, Ástor Piazzolla and Speedy Gonzales, Free Trade and Simón Bolívar, Eva Perón and the Frito Bandito. Just as rejoicing in diversities forms the basis of the work's content, so, too, diversity is the guiding principle of its form.

The broad range of the playwright's dramatic territory is held together by the tension at the heart of his discourse: the dialogue between his two stage personae, "Verdecchia" and "Wideload" (a.k.a. Facundo Morales Segundo). Together these two weave the many narrative, reflective, dialectic, and personal strands of *Fronteras Americanas*. "Wideload," an inflated stereotype designed to deflate stereotypes, is a shrewdly witty commentator. He ponders "Saxonian" attitudes, turns Latino clichés on their sombreros, and even challenges the play itself, offering dramaturgy and criticism from inside the action. He is both a lit match and a safety curtain for the more volatile range of "Verdecchia," and there are no prizes for guessing who *he* is. "Verdecchia's" reflections move from humiliation at the hands of both education and entertainment systems to the shock and horror of what he experiences on his return to South America. Through "Verdecchia," the playwright extends his grasp to the poetic – in the emotional meaning beneath the tango's angularity – and to the mystical – in his spiritual search for integration.

Fronteras Americanas is dazzlingly animated by Guillermo Verdecchia's intelligence, wit, and curiosity. But the satiric, the sardonic, and the ironic are all counterweighted by the extraordinary personal candour of the writing. It is here – in Guillermo Verdecchia's brave commitment to the truth of "Verdecchia" – that the work opens up and absorbs common experiences. Displacement is his theme, with many variations: displacement from one's history, from one's past, from one's surroundings, from oneself. Telling his story, the playwright tells all our stories. How we are torn apart by the conflicting impulses to belong and to remain separate. How we allow ourselves to yield to the same suspicion with which we have been treated. How we want to both stand out and disappear. How we betray ourselves, giving away our very *names* for the quick trade-off of pronunciation ease and acceptance. How we flirt with self-hatred through our fears ("I know that somewhere in my traitorous heart I can't stand people I claim are my brothers").

Guillermo Verdecchia's struggle towards his self shapes the dramatic movement of *Fronteras Americanas*: it is the border within himself that must be crossed. Like all true artists, he embraces the paradox. He takes us with him: "And you? Did you change your name somewhere along the way? Does a part of you live hundred or thousands of kilometres away? Do you have two countries, two memories?" He urges a new geography of the mind and spirit, quoting Octavio Paz: "I am not at the crossroads / to choose / is to go wrong." If uncontrolled displacement was the pattern of the past, *willed* displacement will be the remedy of the future.

URJO KAREDA, July 1993

Preface to the Second Edition

As we were coming down the stairs together at the Young Centre, Albert Schultz, the artistic director of Soulpepper Theatre in Toronto, asked me, "What about doing *Fronteras* here next season?" Albert's charm is difficult to resist, and so, instead of deflecting the question or politely turning down the invitation as I had done in the past, I said I'd think about it.

I wrote and first performed *Fronteras Americanas* a lifetime ago. (Our daughter was born the day the play received the Governor General's Award. She is now in her first year of university.) Writing and performing the play back then was a way to work out some questions that had troubled me for a long time, a way to determine, as I put it in an early grant application, where I lived. After performing the play for a couple of years, I felt like I'd solved the problem. I didn't need the play any longer, so I stopped doing it. Others performed it in Canada and abroad, while I moved on to other questions, other plays.

Still, I found, no matter where I went to work or to speak or to read, many people continued to respond to *Fronteras* and its proposals. Most recently, in Cologne, Germany, a group of students approached me after a reading, among them a young woman from a Turkish family residing in Germany. She was clearly surprised, moved, by what she heard in my reading. She said that the play felt like her experience in Germany, and wanted to know more about it.

I remembered that young woman when I was considering whether or not to mount a production of *Fronteras* at Soulpepper. I also thought of Lukas Podolski, the Polish-born German striker who refused to celebrate his goals against Poland and explained, "I have two hearts beating inside me." Why not do the show again? There are, after all, people all over the globe living, crossing, resisting, defining, and defending linguistic, cultural, racial, gender, psycho-geographical, cartographic, political, and other borders. While the world has changed in many ways since I first wrote and performed *Fronteras*, the processes of migration, displacement, and globalization that informed the play's creation have only accelerated. Some of us may lead more networked lives now, but the Border is alive and well and living all over the globe. The Border trope I stumbled over back then and there remains meaningful, as many kind listeners and audience members have told me.

Director Jim Warren and I spent some time looking at the script before starting rehearsals. We decided the text didn't require a major overhaul, but that there were a few things that could be tweaked for the new production. It felt necessary to acknowledge the moment of the play's writing, the time that had passed since, and the present moment of its enunciation. So I set about tweaking.

But tweaking turned into changes, as it so often does for me. I started with the sorts of emendations I suppose many writers would like to make after their work is published: deleting excesses, trimming unnecessary qualifiers, adjusting rhythms, that sort of thing. Then there were a couple of corrections I wished to make. (What those were I leave to the studious to discover.) I also wanted to update a few pop-culture references: I had to at least mention Sofía Vergara and Javier Bardem, for example. Then I realized I could rewrite a couple of sections to sharpen and complicate a few ideas. All sorts of new images and examples presented themselves for the history section – images and examples that seemed to more apt, more *juste*. And there were new economic relations to consider, new material realities in which Border questions were expressed.

And so we come to the text you are now reading. Kevin Williams, publisher at Talonbooks, and I thought the script had changed enough to merit a new edition. Even so, I don't consider the play finished. The script may be more or less fixed in this new form, but a play (like a Border) is a process, not an object. As before, those choosing to perform *Fronteras* are invited to consider making changes to address the immediate context of their performance and the particular Borders in which they live, not to mention the alignment of the moon, the planets, and the stars.

GUILLERMO VERDECCHIA, July 2012

This version of *Fronteras Americanas* was prepared for the Soulpepper Theatre production, which premiered on May 11, 2011, at the Young Centre for the Performing Arts in Toronto, Ontario, with the following cast and crew:

Performed by Guillermo Verdecchia
Director: Jim Warren
Stage Manager: Alison Peddie
Krista Blackwood: Assistant Stage Manager
Susanne Lankin: Apprentice Stage Manager
Set and Lighting Designer: Glenn Davidson
Projections Designer: Jamie Nesbitt
Sound Designer: Richard Feren
Costume Designer: Ken MacKenzie
Kelly McEvenue: Alexander Coach

Fronteras Americanas was first produced at Toronto's Tarragon Theatre in January and February 1993, with the following cast and crew:

Performed by Guillermo Verdecchia
Director: Jim Warren
Stage Manager: Season Osborne
Designer: Glenn Davidson

Act One

Pre-Show

Music: "Show Me Your Love, America" by James "Blood" Ulmer

Projection (text): It is impossible to say to which human family we belong ... We were all born of one mother America, though our fathers had different origins, and we all have differently coloured skins. This dissimilarity is of the greatest significance.
– Simón Bolívar, Congress of Angostura, 1819

Projection (text): Fronteras Americanas

Projection (text): American Borders

Welcome

VERDECCHIA: Here we are. All together. At long last. Very exciting. I'm excited. Very excited. Here we are.

Projection (text): Here we are

Now, because this is the theatre, when I say "we" I mean all of us, and when I say "here" I don't just mean at Soulpepper Theatre, at the Young Centre; I mean America.

Projection (text): Let us compare geographies

And when I say "AMERICA," I don't mean a country, I mean the continent. Somos todos Americanos. We are all Americans.

Now, I have to make a small confession: I'm lost. Somewhere in my peregrinations on the continent, I lost my way.

Oh sure, I can say I'm in Toronto, in the Distillery District, but that seems to me a rather inadequate description of where I am.

Maps have been of no use because I always forget that maps are metaphors and not the territory. The compass has never made any sense; it always spins in crazy circles. Even gas station attendants haven't been able to help because I can never remember whether it was a right or a left at the lights, and I always miss the exits and have to sleep by the side of the road or in crummy motels that smell of suntan lotion and divorce.

So, I'm lost. And trying to figure out where I took that wrong turn … And I suppose you must be lost, too, or else you wouldn't have ended up here, with me, tonight.

I suspect we got lost while crossing the Border.

Projection (text): Make a run for the border; Taco Bell's got your order

The Border is a tricky place. Take the Mexico-U.S. border.

Projection (image): A map of the Mexico-U.S. border

Where and what exactly is the Border? Is it this line in the dirt, stretching for some three thousand kilometres? Is the Border more accurately described as a zone that includes the towns of El Paso and Juárez? Or is the Border, is the border the whole country, the continent? Where does the U.S. end and Canada begin? Does the U.S. end at the forty-ninth parallel, or does the U.S. only end when you switch on the CBC? After all, as Carlos Fuentes reminds us, a border is more than just the division between two countries; it is also the division between two cultures and two memories.[1]

Atlantic magazine has something to say about the border: "The border is transient. The border is dangerous. The border is crass. The food is bad, the prices are high and there are no good bookstores. It is not the place to visit on your next vacation."[2]

To minimize our inconvenience, I've hired an interpreter who will meet us on the other side.

The border can be difficult to cross. We will have to avoid the border patrol and the trackers who cut for sign.[3] Some of you may wish to put carpet on the soles of your shoes, others may want to attach cow's hooves to their sneakers. I will walk backwards so that it looks like I'm heading north.

Before we cross, please disable any cellular phones or CrackBerrys and reset your watches to Border time. It is now Zero Hour.

El Bandito

> *Music: "Aqui Vienen los Mariachi"*
>
> *Projection (text):* Warning
>
> *Projection (text):* Gunshots will be fired in this performance …
>
> *Projection (text):* NOW

Gunshots sound as FACUNDO enters wearing a bandito costume: dusty poncho with built-in hump, bandoliers, sombrero, moustache, and pistols.

FACUNDO: Ay! Ayayayay! Aja. Bienvenidos. Yo soy el mesonero aquí en La Casa de La Frontera. Soy el guia. A su servicio. Antes de pasar, por favor, los latinos se pueden identificar? Los "latinoamericanos," por favor, que pongan las manos en el aire … (*counting*) Que lindo … mucho gusto … Muy bien. Entonces el resto son … gringos. GUENO, lo siguiente es para los gringos:

Eh, jou en Mejico now. Jou hab crossed de Border. Why? What you lookin' for? Taco Bell nachos wif "salsa sauce," cabron? Forget it, gringo. Dere's no pinche Taco Bell for thousands of miles. Here jou eat what I eat, and I eat raw jalapeño peppers on dirty, burnt tortillas, wif some calopinto peppers to give it some flavour! I drink sewer water and tequila. My breath keells small animals. My shit destroys lakes. Jou come dis far south looking for de authentic Mejico? Jou, señora, you, no doubt, are looking for time-honoured, eco-friendly handicrafts made by the traditional artisans of Chingal Güero Pendejotl? I will take you. Mañana. And jou, señor, jou are looking for de real mezcal wit de real worm in it. I'll show you de real worm. I'll show jou de giant Mexican trouser snake. I will show you fear in a handful of dust …

Bandito maldito, independista, Sandinista, Zapatista. (*waving pistol*) How many bullets are left, Chino? Enough for YOU? Or YOU? All of you! How many can I kill, Chino? How many – and still have one bullet left for me?

FACUNDO fires the pistol and then removes the bandito outfit.

Ees an old Halloween costume. Scary, huh?

Introduction to Wideload

WIDELOAD: Mi nombre es Facundo Morales Segundo. Algunos me llaman El Tigre del Barrio. También me dicen El Alacran …

Music: "La Cumbia del Facundo" by Steve Jordan

My name ees Facundo Morales Segundo. Some of you may know me as de Barrio Tiger. I am de guy who told Elton John to grow some funk of his own. I am de heads of Alfredo García and Joaquin Murrieta. I am a direct descendant of Túpac Amaru, Pancho Villa, Doña Flor, Pedro Navaja, Sor Juana, and Speedy Gonzales.

Now, when I first got here people would say, "Sorry, what's de name? Fuckundoo?"

No, mang, Fa-cun-do, Facundo.

"Wow, dat's a new one. Mind if I call you 'Fac'?"

No, mang. Mind if I call you "shithead"?

So, you know I had to come up with a more Saxonical name. And I looked around for a long time till I found one I liked. And when I found the one I wanted, I took it. I estole it actually from a TV show – *Broken Badge* or something like that? I go by the name Wideload McKennah now, and I get a lot more respect, ese.

Projection (text): Wideload

I live in the Border. That's in Parkdale, for you people from outta town. Ya, mang, I live in de zone, in de barrio, and I gotta move. Is a bad neighbourhood. Dat neighbourhood is going to de dogs. 'Cause dere's a lot of yuppies moving in and dey're wrecking de neighbourhood and making all kinds of noise wif renovating and landscaping, knocking down walls and comparing stained glass. So I gotta move …

But first I gotta make some money. And what I want to do is get a big chunk of toxic wasteland up on de Trans-Canada Highway and make, like, a Third World theme park.

You know, you drive up to, like, big barbed-wire gates with guards carrying submachine guns, and you park your car, and den a broken-down Mercedes-Benz bus comes along and takes you in under guard, of course. And you can buy for 250 dollars an International Monetary Fund credit card that gets you on all de rides.

And as soon as you're inside, somebody steals your purse, and eventually a policeman shows up, but he's totally incompetent, and you have to bribe him in order to get any action. Den you walk through a slum on the edge of a swamp wif poor people selling tortillas. And maybe we'll have a disappearing rainforest section dat you can actually wander through and search for rare plants and maybe find de cure to cancer or maybe find … Sean Connery … and you rent little golf carts to drive through it, and de golf cart is always breaking down, and you have to fix it yourself. And while you're fixing de golf cart in de sweltering noonday sun a drug lord comes along in his hydrofoil and offers to take you to his villa, where you can have lunch and watch a multimedia presentation on drug processing.

I figure it would do great. You people love dat kinda *shit*. And I can undercut dose travel agencies dat are selling adventure tours of Brazilian slums.[4] Dis would be way cheaper, safer, and it would generate a lot of jobs – yeah, for white people, too. And I would make some money and be able to move out of the barrio and into Forest Hill.

Ya, a little house in Forest Hill or Oakville. Nice neighbourhoods. Quiet. Good place to bring, like, fifteen kids. Hey, mang, we could be neighbours! Would you like dat? Sure, I'm moving in next door to … you … and I'm going to work on my ranfla, my low-rider, every day and overhaul de engine and get some grease on your part of de sidewalk. And some friends, like about … twelve, are gonna come and stay with me for a few … years.

You like music? Goood!

Ya, how 'bout a Chicano for a neighbour? Liven up de neighbourhood.

> *Projection (text):* Chicano: The people of Aztlán?
> A generic term for a working-class Latino?
> A Mexican born in Saxon America?
> A person who drives a loud car that sits low to the ground?

Technically I don't qualify as a Chicano. I wasn't born in East L.A. I wasn't born in de southwest USA. I'n not even from Mejico. Does dis make me Hispanic?

> *Projection (text):* Hispanic: A bureaucratic
> euphemism for "brown"?
> A Spaniard?
> A Latino?
> The root of the word "Spic"?

Dese terms, "Latino," "Hispanic," are very tricky, you know, but dey are de only terms we have so we have to use dem wif caution. De term "Latino" is confusing because it lumps a whole lot of different people from thirty countries into one category.[5] And de term "Hispanic" comes from the Roman word for eSpain. eSpain is a country in eEurope. Many people who today are referred to as Hispanic have nothin to do wif Hispain. Some of dem don't even speak Hispanish.

As for me, let's just say ... I'm a pachuco. Y un poco mas chucote que la chingada, carnal![6]

Projection (text): PACHUCO

Music: "Pachuco" by Maldita Vecindad

It Starts

VERDECCHIA: Okay, I just want to stop for a moment before we get all confused.

I've known that I've been lost for quite some time now – years and years, but if I can find the moment that I first discovered I was lost, there might be a clue ...

This all starts with Jorge. Therapy wasn't going so well, so Jorge suggested I go see El Brujo. I wasn't keen on the idea, being both skeptical and afraid of curanderos, but Jorge was persuasive and lent me bus fare enough to get me at least as far as the border ...

It actually starts before that. It starts in France. Paris, France, *The Moveable Feast*, the City of Light, where I lived for a couple of years. En France où mes etudiants me disaient que je parlais le français comme une vache Catalan. En France, où j'étais étranger, un Argentin-Canadien, une faux touriste. Paris, France, where I lived and worked illegally; where, for some reason, known perhaps only by Carlos Gardel and Julio Cortázar, I felt almost at home.

Or it starts before the City of Light, in the City of Sludge: Kitchener, Ontary-airy-airy-o. Kitchener, where I first had sex, where there was nothing to do but eat doughnuts and dream of elsewhere. There in Kitchener, where a stranger once suggested that I go back to my own country.

No. It starts, in fact, at the airport where my parents and my grandparents and our friends couldn't stop crying and hugged each other continually and said goodbye again and again until the stewardess finally came and took me out of my father's arms and carried me onto the plane, forcing my parents to finally board ...

Maybe. Maybe not.

Maybe it starts with Columbus. Maybe it starts with the genius Arab engineer who invented the rudder. Maybe a little history is required to put this all in order.

History

Projection (text): An Idiosyncratic History of America

VERDECCHIA: Our History begins approximately two hundred million years ago in the Triassic period of the Mesozoic era when the original supercontinent, Pangaea, broke up, and the continents of the earth assumed the shapes we now recognize.

Projection (image): A map of the world

Approximately 90,000 BC: A small group of anatomically modern humans leave Africa. All non-African people are descended from this group who spread across Asia and Europe, mingling with Neanderthals and painting caves along the way. They eventually cross the Bering land bridge into the Americas. Some set up camp at Meadowcroft. Others head to Taima-Taima. Still others make for the Distillery District to see *Fronteras Americanas.*

Projection (image): A map of modern human migration

1,200 BC: The Olmec of Meso-America develop a calendar, hieroglyphic writing, and the concept of zero. Most importantly, they cultivate cocoa, so we can have chocolate.

Projection (image): An Olmec head

Early 1400s AD: While Europeans are burning young women like Joan of Arc (*projection [image]: A statue of Joan of Arc*), the Incas have developed a highly efficient political system.

1492: (*projection [image]: A portrait of Christopher Columbus*) This guy sails the ocean blue. Soon the New World is overrun by swineherds and illiterate rogues, the so-called conquistadores, who seek only to amass wealth and live like the lords they suffered under in Spain.

1588: The invincible Spanish Armada is defeated. Spain grows poorer and poorer as gold from the New World is melted down to pay for wars, and imported manufactured goods from the developed northern countries. El Greco finishes *The Burial of the Count of Orgaz.*

Projection (image): The Burial of the Count of Orgaz

1808: France invades Spain, and while the Spaniards are distracted, wars of independence break out all over New Spain. Goya records the French invasion in *The Third of May 1808*.

Projection (image): El Tres de Mayo de 1808

1812: A war breaks out in North America. No one paints anything of note.

1835: U.S. immigrants to the Mexican state of Texas refuse to adapt to Mexican culture and instead start a revolution.[7]

1846: The U.S. attacks Mexico.

1861: France attacks Mexico and later installs an Austrian as emperor.

Projection (image): Maximilian I, Emperor of Mexico

1867: Mexico's Austrian emperor is executed, the first volume of *Das Kapital* is published, and the Dominion of Canada is established. Meanwhile, a Welsh colony has been established in Patagonia, with the assistance of the Tehuelche and Mapuche people.

1902 and 1903: Gorky writes *The Lower Depths*, the U.S. acquires control over the Panama Canal, and Beatrix Potter writes *Peter Rabbit*.

Projection (image): Peter Rabbit

1922: Canadian Mennonites, prohibited from speaking German in Manitoba schools, move to Chihuahua, Mexico.[8]

1938: César Vallejo, the Peruvian poet, dies in Paris, as he predicted he would. He dies thinking of Spain.

Projection (image): César Vallejo

1940: After much pleading from my grandmother, my grandfather agrees to take her to the cinema on his one day off. They dress up to see the new Hollywood import *Argentine Nights*, which is the screen debut of the Andrews Sisters.

We hear a burst of "Boogie Woogie Bugle Boy" by the Andrews Sisters.

Unfortunately, the depiction of Argentina as a ridiculous tropical country causes a riot in the theatre. My grandmother's smart new hat is crushed in the fracas, and my grandparents never go to the cinema together again.

We hear the intro to "Tanga" by Mario Bauzá.

1947: Mario Bauzá writes "Tanga," John Birks "Dizzy" Gillespie meets Chano Pozo, Stan Kenton hears Machito. Afro-Cuban jazz is born.

1961: *West Side Story* (*projection [image]: A photo of the "Sharks" in mid-dance*) wins ten Academy Awards, a 680-pound giant sea bass is caught off the Florida coast (*projection [image]: A photo of a large fish*), and the U.S. sponsors an attack on Cuba (*projection [image]: A photo of Fidel Castro*).

1969: Ravi Shankar, Carlos Santana, and Jimi Hendrix play Woodstock; Richard Nixon (*projection [image]: A photo of Nixon*) becomes president of the U.S.; Samuel Beckett (*projection [image]: A photo of Beckett*) wins the Nobel Prize for Literature; the Montreal Canadiens (*projection [image]: A photo of the Canadiens in 1969*) win the Stanley Cup for hockey; and I attend my first day of classes at Anne Hathaway Public School.

Roll Call

Music: "God Save the Queen"

VERDECCHIA: I am seven years old. The teacher at the front of the green classroom reads names from a list.

"Jonathan Kramer?"

Jonathan puts his hand up. He is a big boy with short red hair.

"Sandy Nemeth?"

Sandy puts her hand up. She is a small girl with long hair. When she smiles we can see the gap between her front teeth.

"Michael Uffelman?"

Michael puts his hand up. He is a tall boy with straight brown hair who is sitting very neatly in his chair.

My name is next.

Minutes, hours, a century passes as the teacher, Miss Wiseman, forces her mouth into shapes hitherto unknown to the human race as she attempts to pronounce my name.

"Gwillyou-rellye-moo ... Verdeek-cheea?"

I put my hand up. I am a minuscule boy with ungovernable black hair, antennae and gills where everyone else has a mouth.

You can call me "Willy," I say. The antennae and gills disappear.

It could have been here – but I don't want to talk about myself all night.

Wideload's Terms

WIDELOAD: Thank God.

I mean, I doan know about you, but I hate it when I go to el teatro – to de theatre – and I am espectin to see a play, and instead I just get some guy up dere talking about himself – deir life story – who cares? Por favor …

And what kind of play is this anyway? No plot, no central character. No fourth wall. That is shoddy construction. You people are totally unprotected.

But at least you're in de Distillery. Doan you love de Distillery Districk? Yeah, man, it's super-chevere. Is my favourite place to get really … expensive chocolate. It's also a great place to observe Saxons doing what they do best: shopping among the ruins of an older civilization. But it's funny, you know; this is a place where people used to make things. Real things, not websites. We used to call a person who did that a worker.

Projection (text): WORKER

Say it with me: "WORKER." We still have workers, but they are mostly in the Third World, part of which is farther up Sherbourne Street. So, people used to make things here, and now, people buy things here. And part of what they buy is the nostalgic backdrop of industrial production.

And that in a nutshell, for those who were wondering, is late capitalism.[9]

But you didn't come to Schultzpepper for this post-Marxist disparate and you certainly didn't come to hear about stuff that's going on TODAY! So, let me tell you a little about myself …

When I first got to America del Norte, I needed a place to live, and I diden have a lot of money, so I stayed wif a family. The Smiths – Mr. and Mrs. and deir two kids, Cindy and John. And it was nice, you know. Like, it was, like, my first contact with an ethnic family, and I got a really good look at de way dey live. I mean, sure, at times it was a bit exotic for me, you know, de food, for example: Macaroni Majestic? But mostly I just realized they were a family like any other, wif crazy aunts and communication problems and onerous personal and household debt, and a dog named Buster dat ate my socks.

Dey wanted to know all about me, so I told dem stories about my mafioso uncle El Gato, and how he won a tank and his wife in a poker game; and stories about my aunt, the opera singer, Luisa la Sonrisa; and about my cousing, Esperanza, about her Border crossings and how she almost fell in love.

I came here for a Metallica concert, and I liked it so much here, I decided to stay and do some studies. Thanks to my cousing Esperanza, who always used to say to me, "You should learn to use your brain or someone else will use it for you," I now have an advanced degree in avant-garde geography. Simónese. I do some work with a consortium of experimental cartographers, mapping the flow of deterritorialized memories among migrant farm workers in Leamington. And I recently founded the *Chico and the Man* Re-enactment Society.

Music: "Chico and the Man (Theme)" by José Feliciano

We just held our first annual symposium, which I dedicated to my cousing Esperanza back home.[10]

Going Home

VERDECCHIA: To go home. The idea preyed on me when I was younger but, apparently, I had committed treason by neglecting to register for military service in Argentina when I was sixteen, even though I was living in Canada. And, consequently, everybody insisted that the minute I stepped off a plane in Buenos Aires, military policemen would spring from the tarmac, arrest me, and guide me to a jail cell where they would laugh at my earrings and give me a proper haircut.

> *Projection (image): A photo of a younger*
> *VERDECCHIA, wearing earrings and needing*
> *a haircut*

I phoned the consulate one day to try to get the official perspective on my situation. I gave a false name, and I explained that I wanted to go HOME for a visit, that I was now a Canadian citizen, and no, I hadn't registered for my military service. The gentleman at the consulate couldn't tell me exactly what my status was, but he suggested that I come down to the consulate, where they would put me on a plane, which would fly me directly to Bs. As., where I would appear before a military tribunal who could tell me in no uncertain terms what my status actually was.

"Well, I'll certainly consider that," I said.

And I waited seven years. And in those seven years, the military government is replaced by a civilian one and I decide I can wait no longer; I will risk a return HOME. I set off to discover the Southern Cone.

To minimize my risk, I apply for a new Canadian passport that does not list my place of birth.

Projection (image): Passport photos

And I plan to fly first to Santiago, Chile, and then cross the border in a bus that traverses the Andes and goes to Mendoza, Argentina.

After an absence of almost fifteen years, I am *going home*. Even now, so many years later, the words "going home" feel like a lovely, half-remembered dream, but then, at the tender age of twenty-six, "going home" became my mantra.

Going Home. I am Going Home. All will be resolved, dissolved, revealed. I will claim my place in the universe when I Go Home.

Music: "Vuelvo Al Sur" by Gotan Project[11]

I had spent fifteen years preparing for this. Buying records and studying the liner notes. Drinking maté, eating dulce de leche. Talking to my friends, questioning my parents, and practising Spanish with strangers. I befriended former Montonero and Tupamaro guerrillas and people even more apocryphal, like Jorge: painter, serious smoker. Jorge, who moved to Italy and left me alone with my memories. I tracked down a Salvador Allende poster, found postcards of Che and Pablo Neruda. I drank Malbec wines and black market pisco. I saw the movie *Missing* three times.

Santiago

VERDECCHIA: Santiago, Chile.

Chile, as your *Fodor's* travel guide will tell you, immediately strikes the visitor as very cosmopolitan, and is known for its award-winning wines and excellent seafood. Chileans, *Fodor's* tell us, are a handsome, stylish people known for their openness and hospitality. My 1989 *Fodor's* also tells me that under Pinochet, Chile enjoys a more stable political climate than it did in the early seventies, but reports persist of government-sponsored assassinations, kidnappings, and torture. Tell me about it, man, I saw *Missing* (three times).

Well, it is now 1990, and the horrific Pinochet dictatorship is a thing of the (recent) past. I ride a comfortable bus into Santiago and continue reading my *Fodor's*, which tells me, "Unfortunately, South America's democracies seem to have higher street-crime rates than the police states." I guess assassination, kidnapping, and torture don't count as street crime. I look out the window and read the graffiti: Ojo! La derecha no duerme. I count all the policemen: one per block, it seems. What was it like under Pinochet? A policeman in every home?

Tired from a ten-hour flight, I check into the Hotel de Don Tito, listed on page 302 of your *Fodor's* as a moderate, small hotel, with a bar and homey atmosphere, and it's located on one of the main streets in Santiago – Huerfanos – at Huerfanos 578 ("Huerfanos": Spanish for "orphans"). I shower, shave, and take an afternoon nap.

Three blasts from the street wake me up and pull me to the window.

Music: "Jingo" by Santana

There, three stories below, directly in front of the moderate and homey Hotel de Don Tito, there on the road, directly below my window, there a man in a suit, his shirt soaked an impossible red, lies writhing as an enormous crowd gathers. I reach for my camera and begin to take photographs. I take photographs with a 135 mm telephoto and then change lenses to get a sense of the crowd that has built up. I take photographs of the man who was shot on the first day of my return home after an absence of almost fifteen years, as more policemen arrive, pulling weapons from their jean jackets. I take photographs as the man in the suit, his lower body apparently immobilized, reaches wildly for the legs that surround him, as the motorcycle police expertly push the crowd away from the Hotel de Don Tito, moderate in *Fodor's*, Huerfanos 578, homey, page 302. I take photographs as still more policemen arrive waving things that look like Uzis. I take photographs with a Pentax MX and a 35 mm f/2.8 lens as the dying man, one of his shoes lying beside him, his gun on the road, gives up reaching for the legs around him. I take photographs from my room in the Hotel de Don Tito, Huerfanos 578, moderate in *Fodor's*, as the press arrives and NO AMBULANCE EVER COMES. I take photographs, ASA 64 Kodachromes, as he dies and I take photographs as the policemen (all men) talk to each other and I wonder if anyone has seen me and I take photographs as the policemen smoke cigarettes and cover him up and I take photographs and I realize that I have willed this to happen.

Dancing

WIDELOAD: Oye, you know I do like you Saxons. Really, you guys are great. I always have a very good time whenever we get together. Though sontines, I'll be out with some friends from de Saxonian community, and we'll be having a few cervezas, you know, vacilando and some music will be playing, and "La Bamba" will come on. And all de Saxons get all excited and start tappin deir toes, and some get all carried away and start doing dis thing with deir heads (*he demonstrates the bobblehead action Saxons make when they listen to lively music*) … and dey get dis look in deir eyes like it's Christmas, an dey look at me and say, "Hey, Wideload, 'La Bamba.'"

Ya, mang, la puta bamba.

"Wideload, man, do you know de words?"

Do I know de words?

Mang, do I have an enorme pinga? Of course I know de words: Pala pala pala la Bamba ... Who doesn't know de words?

Music: "Navidad Negra" by Ramiro's Latin Orchestra

Espeaking of music I haf to say dat I love de way you guys dance. I think you Saxons are some of de most interesting dancers on de planet. I lof to go down to the club when my friend Ramiro is playing and just watch you guys dance because you are so free – like nothing gets in your way: not de beat, not de rhythm, nothing.

What I especially like to watch is, like, a Saxon guy dancing wif a Latin woman. Like, she is out dere and she's smiling and doing a little cu-bop step and she's having a good time and de Saxon guy is like trying really hard to keep up. You know, he's making a big effort to move his hips independently of his legs and rib cage and he's flapping his arms like a flamenco dancer. Generally speaking dis applies just to the male Saxon. Saxon women seem to have learned a move or two.

Of course part of de problem is dat you guys wear very funny shoes for dancing – dose giant running shoes with built-in air compressors. You might as well try dancing wif snowshoes on. Your feet have got to be free, so dat your knees are free, so dat your hips are free, so dat you can move your culo wif impunity.

So dere dey are dancing away: de Saxon guy and de Latin woman or de Saxon woman and de Latin guy, and you can see de Saxon thinking, "Wow, he (or she) can really dance, he (or she) can really move dose hips, he (or she) keeps smiling, I think she (or he) likes me, I bet she (or he) would be great in bed …"

Now. Dis is important, so I'm going to continue talking about it even though it always gets real quiet whenever I start in on this stuff.

The fact is that whenever a Latin and a Saxon have sex, it is going to be a mind-expanding and culturally enriching experience. Porque nosotros sabemos hacer cosas que ni se imaginaron en la Kama Sutra, mang, porque nosotros tenemos un ritmo, un calor, un sabor, un tumbao de timbale, de conga, de candomble, de kilombo. Una onda, un un dos tres, un dos. Saben …?

Dose of you who want a translation of dat come and see me after de show or ask one of de eSpanish espeakers in de audience at intermission.

Now, I doan want you to get de impression I'm picking on you Saxons. Nothing could be further from my mind. I have de greatest respect for your culture … and, you know, every culture has its own fertility dances, its own dance of sexual joy. You people, you Saxons hab de Morris dance.

Projection (video): Morris dancers

Dis is a very sexy dance. You know. A buncha guys get together, dress up like leprechauns, hop aroun' wif bells on deir ankles, and swing sticks at each other. And hey, you go to a Morris dance festival, and it's de Latinos who look silly. You have de

Morris dance – and we have de mambo, de rumba, de cumbia, de son, de tango, de samba, salsa, reggaeton … shall I continue?

Latin Lovers

WIDELOAD: Latin lovers.

Projection (image): A photo of Antonio Banderas

Almost as old as de movies, de Latin lover is always being reincarnated. When Antonio Banderas made his Hollywood breakthrough, *Elle* magazine announced: "A Latin Love God Is Born."

Projection (image): Elle magazine cover

Sometimes de Latin lover is reborn as a woman.

Projection (image): A photo of Dolores del Río

Dolores del Río. She was Mexican, but the Hollywood press made a big deal of her "ivory skin" and "Spanish ancestry" because being Mexican back then wasn't as cool as it is now.

Rita Cansino.

Projection (image): A photo of Rita Hayworth

Or perhaps you know her as Rita Hayworth? She changed her name, her hairline, and hair colour to become the GIs' favourite pin-up girl.

Projection (image): A photo of Maria Montez

Maria Montez. Some of you may remember her as Cobra Woman from Cobra Island. Dat's not a real place.

Projection (image): A photo of Rita Moreno

Rita Moreno. She's from Puerto Rico. Dat is a real place.

Projection (image): A photo of Carmen Miranda

Sure, Carmen Miranda.

Not exactly a lover, but the image of good times anywhere down south, though she was Brazilian. Smiling, sexy even with all dose goddamned bananas on her head, she ended up unemployable, blacklisted because a certain Senator McCarthy found her obscene.

Today we have Sofía Vergara.

Projection (image): A photo of Sofía Vergara

She has fantastic … earrings.

Salma Hayek.

Projection (image): A photo of Salma Hayek

She also has great jewellery.

And Penélope Cruz.

Projection (image): A photo of Penélope Cruz

AI! MAMI!

For de men dere was Rudolph Valentino (*projection [image]: A photo of Rudolph Valentino*); Ramon Novarro (*projection [image]: A photo of Ramon Novarro*); Ricardo Cortez, real name: Jakob Kranz! (*projection [image]: A photo of Ramon Novarro*).

Projection (image): A photo of Fernando Lamas

Fernando Lamas. He was Argentinian.

Projection (image): A photo of Ricardo Montalbán

Ricardo Montalbán. "Welcome to Fantasy Island." Also known as "Khaan!"

Projection (image): A photo of Desi Arnaz

And Desi Arnaz, whom we all remember as Ricky Ricardo from Ricky and Lucy, those all-time great TV lovers. Now, Ricky may not live up to de steamy image of unbridled sexuality we expect from our Latin lovers, but you have to admit he's a pretty powerful icon. Funny, cute, musical, and more often dan not ridiculous.

Most recently, we have Antonio Banderas, Gael García Bernal, Benicio del Toro, and Javier Bardem.

Projections (images): Photos of Banderas, García Bernal, del Toro, and Bardem

And dere's been a lot of excitable ink spilled over dese guys in newspapers and magazines.

Projection (image): Cover of GQ magazine featuring Javier Bardem

Here's one for example. The subtitle here says, "De Return of Macho." (*pause*) Did macho go away for a while? I hadn't noticed. Anyway, it's back for dose of you who missed it.

And it doesn't matter if they're writing about Banderas, García Bernal, or Bardem, these articles always say pretty much the same thing. Let's see, shall we, what *Elle* magazine has to say about the Latin lover?

(*reading from* Elle) "He's short, dark, and handsome, with lots of black hair from head to chest. He's wildly emotional, swinging from brooding sulks to raucous laughter and singing loudly in public. He's relentlessly romantic, with a fixation on love that looks to be total: he seems to be always about to shout, 'I must have you.'"[12]

> *Projection (text):* I must have you

"He is the Latin lover, an archetype of masculinity built for pleasure."

These articles begin by explaining the myth of the Latin lover, and then use the myth to explain Banderas, García Bernal, or Bardem, who, apparently, cannot explain demselves because their Inglich is too limited. All the articles mention their accents and the adorable mistakes they make.

This magazine (*projection [image]: Another women's fashion magazine cover*) describes in fond detail how Bardem pronounces the word "L-O-V-E." He pronounces it "looov-aaa." Ooooh isn't dat sweet and sexy, and don't you just want to wrap him up in your arms and let him whisper filthy things in your ear in Spanish and broken English? Especially when, as also described in the article, he wipes his mouth on the tablecloth and asks, "What can I done?" Don't you just want to fuck him? I do. I wonder though if it would be quite so disarming or charming if it was Fidel Castro wiping his mouth on the tablecloth?

And dese articles often mention de casting challenges, because sometimes de estudio doesn't want to hire some guy who wipes his mouth on the tablecloth; they want a name – a big-name, A-list actor – like Adam Sandler – to play de Mexican desperado. But the article tells us that the director of the movie had the "cajones" (*projection [text]:* Cajones) to buck the studio and give the part to Bardem. (*beat*) Cajones …

Now, the word I think they want to use is "cojones" (*projection [text]:* Cojones), which is a colloquial term for testicles. What they've ended up with here is a sentence that means the director had the *crates* or *drawers* to buck the studio.

> *Projection (text):* Cojones = testicles
> Cajones = crates

Could be just a typo, but you never know.

It's not as silly as it might seem. For me, it's about this business of Latin lovers being archetypes of men and women built for pleasure. But where did this archetype come from and WHOSE pleasure are we talking about, mang? Your movie-going pleasure? The pleasure of de Hollywood-industrial complex? Think about it.

In dose movies, we can't solve our own problems, we can't win a revolution without help from gringos, we can't build the pyramids at Chichen Itza without help from space aliens, and we don't win the Nobel Prize. No. Instead we sing, we dance, we fuck like a dream, we die early on, we sleep a lot, we speak funny, we cheat on each other, we get scared easy, and we amuse you. And please don't tell me it's just a movie. Because every movie, no matter how stupid, always makes some proposal, has some kind of –

> *WIDELOAD is interrupted by the sound of a loud buzzer.*

Dere goes de buzzer, indicating dat approximately fifty minutes of de show have already elapsed and dat less dan fifteen minutes remain till intermission. Unofficial tests indicate dat local audiences grow restless at de fifty-minute mark, so we are going to take a little break and give you de opportunity to shift around in your seats, and whisper to de person next to you, look in de program, and try to figure out what the hell is going on. You can also use this time to scratch your culo.

And during dis break we are gonna see some clips from a mega-musical spectacular dat will be opening here soon. It's called *Our Pueblo*. Is a musical about a group of Chilean miners, and they are gonna be building a special theatre to house this show. Is gonna be underground, and you are gonna be trap down dere with them. Is truly authentic. Is gonna be an adobe theatre with adobe sound.

Here's de break.

> *Projection (video): Clips of cartoons and movies featuring, among other things, Latinos, Hispanics, dopey peasants, perhaps Emiliano Zapata as played by Marlon Brando, and a certain famously fast mouse. Music: "Speedy Gonzales" by Pat Boone. The video clip concludes, and we hear the loud buzzer again.*

Travel Sickness

VERDECCHIA: When I travel I get sick. I've thrown up in most of the major centres of the Western world: Paris, Rome, Madrid, New York, London, Venice, Calgary ... And it's not just too much to drink or drugs; sometimes it's as simple as the shape of the clouds in the sky, or the look someone gives me in the market, or the sound my shoes make on the street. These things are enough to leave me shaking and sweating in bed with a churning stomach, no strength in my legs, and unsettling dreams.

Well, I'm in Bs. As., and so far, I haven't thrown up. So far, *everything's fine*.

We meet in Caballito. And Alberto and I have dinner in a bright, noisy restaurant called The Little Pigs and *everything's fine*. And now we're looking for some place to hear some music, a place in San Telmo to hear some contemporary music, not tango and not folklore; Alberto wants to go see a band called Little Balls of Ricotta and *everything's fine* but first we have to get the flat tire on his uncle's Fiat fixed. We stop at a gomeria, a garage, where they fix tires. I'm feeling like I need some air so I get out of the car and *everything's fine*; I'm looking for Alberto but can only see a guy scrupulously cleaning a tire with a dirty rag. I'm leaning over the car and suddenly I feel very hot and awful and just as quickly I feel better. I wake up and I'm sitting on the road and somebody's thrown up on me; then I realize the vomit is my own and I'm in Buenos Aires and I'm sick and we're in a tricky part of town and the cops will be passing by any minute and I haven't done my military service –

Alberto puts me in the back of the car.

We drive back to my apartment (not mine actually, my grandmother's, but she's not there for some reason, and I'm using it). I'm feeling a little better but weak, can't raise my head; I watch Buenos Aires spin and speed past and around me, through the back window, like a movie I think, "Yeah, that's it, I'm in a Costa-Gavras film."

I leave tomorrow, back to Canada, and I ruined this last evening by getting sick, I can't fly like this all poisoned, and for some reason I remember Alberto telling me how by the end of the month people are coming to his store on the edge of a villa, on the edge of slum,[13] and asking if they can buy one egg or a quarter of a package of butter or a few cigarettes and I think, "Yes, in a few years we will kill for an apple and I throw up in the bidet and I just want to go home – but I'm already there – aren't I?" Eventually, I crawl into my grandmother's bed and sleep.

Music: "Asleep" by Ástor Piazzolla, performed by Kronos Quartet

I dream of Mount Aconcagua, of Iguazu, of Ushuaia and condors, of the sierras – yellow and green, of orange, quebracho, and ombu trees, of running, sweating horses, of café cortado served with little glasses of soda water, of the smell of Particulares 30, of the vineyards of Mendoza, of barrels full of ruby-red vino tinto, of gardens as beautiful as Andalusia in spring. I dream of thousands of emerald-green parrots flying alongside my airplane – parrots just like the ones that flew alongside the bus as I travelled through the interior.

The Other

VERDECCHIA: I would like to clear up any possible misimpression. I should state now that I am something of an impostor. A fake. What I mean is I sometimes confuse my tenses in Spanish. I couldn't dance a tango to save my life.

All sides of the Border have claimed and rejected me. On all sides I have been asked, "How long have you been …? How old were you when …? When did you leave? When did you arrive?" As if it were somehow possible to locate on a map, on an airline schedule, on a blueprint, the precise coordinates of the spirit, of the psyche, of memory.

Music: "El Mal Dormido" by Atahualpa Yupanqui

As if we could somehow count or measure these things.

These things cannot be measured – I know I tried.

I told the doctor, "I feel different. I feel wrong, out of place. I feel not-nowhere, not-neither."

The doctor said, "You're depressed."

I said, "Yes, I am."

The doctor said, "Well …"

I said, "I want to be tested. Sample my blood, scan my brain, search my organs. Find it."

"Find what?"

"Whatever it is."

"And when we find it?"

"Get rid of it."

Projections (images): X-rays, brain scans, MRIs

They didn't find anything. "Everything's absolutely normal," I was told. "Everything's fine. Everything's where it should be." I wasn't fooled. I am a direct descendant of two people who once ate armadillo. Armadillo has a half-life of two thousand years; you can't tell me that isn't in my bloodstream. Evita Perón once kissed my mother, and that night she felt her cheek begin to rot. You can't tell me that hasn't altered my DNA.

El Teatro

WIDELOAD: Let's turn on de lights, see who came to el teatro dis evening.

Chucha! Look at all de white people! Is so inneresting ...
Errywhere you go in this city, the subway, the bank, the Office
of Boating Safety, is like, you know, the United Nations. But go
to the theatre – nothing but white people in all directions. What
is that about? Is so ... antiquated. Is almost charming. But look
out. 'Cause you get this many white people together in one
place, and anything can happen: like a book launch could break
out at any moment. Or a monster truck rally ... No, but you
people have been very well behave. You are a credit to your
race.[14]

Are you a group? Do you know each other? No, well, some of
you know de person next to you, but collectively you are
strangers. Estrangers in de Night. But perhaps by the end of the
evening you will no longer be strangers because you will have
shared an experience, carnal. You will have gone through dis
show together, and it will have created a common bond among
you, a common reference point.

That's the theory anyway. That the theatre is valuable because a
bunch of strangers come together and share an experience. But
is it true? I mean, how can you be sharing an experience when
you are all (thankfully) different people? You have different jobs,
different genders, different histories, different sexual
orientations. You are all watching dis show from a different
perspective. Most of you, for example, have been awake.

Who knows what is really going on here? I mean, some of you
are from Thornhill, some perhaps from el Caribe, most of you

clearly from eScandinavia, and you all ended up in dis room with me. And me, I left home to escape poverty, and I ended up working in de theatre? Weird. Let's take a break, huh?

It's intermission, ladies and gentlemen. Get your refrescos and Wideload collectibles outside. Órale, pues!

Music: "Hombre Secreto (Secret Agent Man)" by the Plugz

Acto Segundo

Living Border

> *Projection (image):* América Invertida (1943) *by Joaquín Torres García*
>
> *Projection (text):* Some say that these lands were first known many centuries ago, and that their situation was written down and the exact latitude noted in which they lay but their geography and the sea routes by which they were to be reached were forgotten ...[15]
>
> *Music: "Peligro" by Mano Negra*

Call to Arms

VOICEOVER: Ladies and gentlemen, this play is not a plea for tolerance. This is not a special offer for free mambo lessons nor an invitation to order discount Starbucks Rhythms of the World CDs. This is a manifesto, a citation. This is a summons to renegotiate your place on the continent.

Of Ferrets and Avocados

WIDELOAD: NEVER GIVE A FERRET AVOCADO!

Projection (image): A photo of a ferret

De ferret ees a Northern European animal – known also as de polecat and related to de bear and de wolberine. Dey are fierce little creatures, used to kill pests like rabbits. De ferret can be domesticated. Some of you may have a ferret of your own which you have affectionately named Blinky or Squiggly or Beowulf. It takes four generations to domesticate a ferret but only one generation for the ferret to revert to a feral state. Dat means to go savage. Inneresting, huh?

De avocado is a fruit from de southern hemisphere known as avocado, aguacate, and palta. It is rich and nutritious and can be used in all sorts of ways – as a mayonnaise, in guacamole, spread some on some pork tenderloin for a sanwich Cubano. Avocados make lousy pets. Dey are not playful and do not respond at all to commands.

Never give a ferret avocado.

Because it will blow up. Deir northern constitutions cannot process de rich southern fruit.

Think about dat.

Music: "Atrévete-te-te" by Calle 13

WIDELOAD struts down and across the stage, showing and taking off his zoot suit jacket, tie, hat, etc. He stops abruptly.

Correction

WIDELOAD: I want to draw some attention to myself. Some more attention. I want to talk about dat nasty *S*-word: "estereotype." I would like to set the record straight on dis subject and state dat I am by no means an estereotype. At least I am no more of an estereotype dan dat other person in de show: dat neurotic Argentinian. And I know dere's a lot of confusion on dis subject, so let me offer a few pointers.

If I was a real estereotype, I wouldn't be aware of it. I wouldn't be talking to you about being an estereotype. If I was a real estereotype, you would be laughing at me, not with me. And if I was a real estereotype, you wouldn't take me seriously. And you do take me seriously. Don't you?

Border Crossings

VERDECCHIA: Los Angeles. Uh, Los, Las Anngel – Lows Anjelees, uh, L.A.

A week.

Pleasure.

I'm a Canadian citizen.

Pleasure. (Didn't I just answer that question?)

I'm … an … I work in the theatre, actually.

No, not a movie theatre, I work in The Theatre. I do plays? I do theatre (*miming a wall*) plays?

I don't think you would have heard – Okay, uh, uh, Canadian Stage, the Tarragon, Soulpepper – I'm not surprised.

I told you: pleasure. Come on, what is this? I'm a Canadian citizen – we're supposed to be friends. You know, Free Trade, the longest undefended border in the world … all that? (I had less trouble getting into Argentina.)

Some borders are easier to cross than others. Try starting a conversation in Vancouver with the following statement: "I like Toronto."

Some things cross borders more easily than others.

Money can cross borders in an instant. Certain kinds of people, though – poor Guatemalans, for example; Palestinians; and people with names that sound like "Ahmadinejad" – they don't cross quite so easily.

Projection (image): A large, angry bee

Killer bees, on the other hand, respect no political or cartographic boundary.

Music: "Muiñeira de Villanova" by Milladoiro

Music. Music crosses borders.

My grandfather was a gallego, from Galicia, Spain. This music is from Galicia, and yes, those are bagpipes. Those of us with an ethnomusicological bent can only ask ourselves, "How did the bagpipes ever end up in … Scotland?"

Ponte guapa que traen el haggis!

The bandoneón, cousin to the concertina and stepbrother to the accordion, came to the Río de la Plata via Germany. Originally intended for organless churches, the bandoneón found its true calling in the dives of Buenos Aires and Montevideo playing the most profane music of all: the tango.

Banned by Pope Pius X, the tango was, at first, often danced only by men because its postures were considered too crude, too sexual for women – it was, after all, one of the first dances in which men and women embraced.

Ludwig II of Bavaria forbade his officers to dance it, and the Duchess of Norfolk explained that the tango was (*with a posh English accent*) "contrary to English character and manners," but the tango, graciously received in the salons of Paris, soon swept London's Savoy hotel and the rest of Europe. Finally, even Argentina's upper classes acknowledged it.

The tango, however, has not been entirely domesticated. It is impossible to shop or aerobicize to tango … porque el tango es un sentimiento triste que se baila.

And what is it about the tango, this binational treasure that some say was born of the gaucho's crude attempts to waltz?

Music: "Verano Porteño" by Ástor Piazzolla

It is music for exile, for the preparations, the significations of departure, for the symptoms of migration. It is the languishing music of picking through your belongings and deciding what to take. It is the 2:00 a.m. music of smelling and caressing books, none of which you can carry – books you leave behind with friends who say they'll always be here when you want them, when you need them. Music for a bowl of apples sitting on your table, apples you have not yet eaten, apples you cannot take. You know, they have apples there in that other place, but not these apples – not apples like these. You eat your last native apple and stare at what your life is reduced to – all the things you can stick into a sack. It will be cold – you will need boots – you don't own boots except these rubber ones – will they do? You pack them, you pack a letter from a friend, so you will not feel too alone.

Music for final goodbyes, for one last drink and a quick hug as you cram your cigarettes into your pocket and run to the bus; you run, run, your chest heaves like the bellows of the bandoneón. You try to watch intently, to emblazon in your mind these streets, these corners, those houses, the people, the smells, even the lurching bus fills you with a kind of stupid happiness and regret – music for the things you left behind in that room: a dress, magazines, some drawings, two pairs of shoes, and blouses too old to be worn anymore. Four perfect apples.

Music for cold nights under incomprehensible stars, for cups of coffee and cigarette smoke, for a long walk by the river where you might be alone or you might meet someone. It is music for encounters in shabby stairways, the music of lovemaking in a narrow bed, the tendernesses, the caress, the pull of strong arms and legs.

Music for men and women thin as bones.

Music for your invisibility.

Music for a letter that arrives telling you that he is very sick, music for your arms that ache from longing, from wishing he might be standing at the top of the stairs, waiting to take the bags and then lean over and kiss you, and even his silly stubble scratching your cold face would be welcome, and you only discover that you're crying when you try to find your keys –

Music for a day in the fall when you buy a new coat and think perhaps you will live here for the rest of your life; perhaps it will be possible; you have changed so much – would they recognize you? Would you recognize your country? Would you recognize yourself?

* * *

WIDELOAD: Basically, tango is music for fucked-up people.

* * *

Drug War Deconstruction

WIDELOAD: Hey, I want to show you a little movie. It's a home movie. It came into my home, and I saved it to share with my friends. It's called *The War on Drugs*. Some of you may have seen it already, so we're just gonna watch some of de highlights.

> Projection (video): Edited clips of drug-war
> TV movie

(*watching the video*) Dis is de title. It says, "De War on Drugs." In Big Block Letters. In English. Dis is another title, *The Cocaine Cartel*. Dey're talking about de Medellín Cartel in Colombia.

Dis is de hero. He is a drug enforcement agent from de U.S. who is sent to Colombia to take on de Medellín Cartel. He is smiling. He kisses his ex-wife. Awkwardly. Oh … he is shy.

Dis woman is a kind of judge – a Colombian judge – and she agrees to prosecute de Medellín Cartel, to build a case against de drug lords even though her life is being threatened here on de phone, even as we watch. Watch. (*as the character onscreen speaks*) "But ... I didn't order a pizza."

Dis guy is a jounalist, an editor for a big Colombian newspaper. He is outspoken in his criticism of the drug lords. He has written editorial after editorial condemning de cartel and calling for de arrest of de drug lords. He is a family man, as we can tell by his Volvo car and by de presents which he loads into de car to take to his loved ones.

Okay, dis is a boring sequence, so we can fast-forward through this part (*the video speeds up*).

He's going home after a hard day at de office. Oh. Two guys on a motorcycle. They are in traffic. Driving kind of recklessly. Dey come to an intersection (*the video resumes normal speed*).

Dey estop. De light is red. De guy gets off de motorcycle. Dum-dee-bumbe dum. He has a gun! Oooh! And de family man editor is killed, and as we can see he is driving one of dose Volvos wif de built-in safety feature dat when de driver is killed, de car parks itself automatically. Very good cars, Volvos.

Dis is de Medellín Cartel. Dese are de drug lords. Dey are de bad guys. We know dey are bad because dey have manicured hands, expensive suits, and ... dark hair. Dere's a lot of dem; dey are at a meeting, talking business. And dis guy is de kingpin, Pablo Escobar, head of de Medellín Cartel, de baddest of de bad. We know he is bad because he has reptilian eyes.

Okay, let's put dis on pause for a second. Dis movie shows us a lot of things. It shows us dat drugs wreck families. In dis case de family of de nice white guy who is trying to stop de drug dealers. Nobody in his family uses drugs. It's just he spends so much time fighting drugs dat his family falls apart.

De movie also shows us dat de drug lords are nasty people who will not hesitate to kill anybody who gets in deir way. And de big guy, de kingpin, Pablo Escobar, who is now dead, was according to de *Economist* magazine one of the richest men in the world. Escobar was also a big philanthropist. Interesting, huh? Today, it's de Mexican cartels we're worried about. Like Pablo Escobar before them, they are not only giants in free-market capitalism, they are also very big in public works, especially public housing. Dese movies don't show us dat. What else don't dese movies show us?

Dey don't show us that since NAFTA, 30 percent of the Mexican population tries to stay alive by shining shoes, squeegeeing windows, or selling pencils on the street. Dey don't show us that the formal economy cares even less than the government, and that in some parts of Mexico (or Colombia), drug lords are tolerated or respected because they provide schools, hospitals, churches, homes, and jobs.

Dese movies don't show us that the Bank of America, Citigroup, and other banks made a fortune laundering drug money.

Don't show us dat money from de sale of drugs was used to fund the U.S. Contra war on Nicaragua that left thirty thousand Nicaraguans dead.[16]

They don't show – but perhaps I've gone on enough. After all, you people don't watch propaganda like this; you are good people who patronize the theatre … And I'm sure that whenever you stick a straw up your nose, or light up a spliff of Acapulco Gold you know exactly where the money you give your dealer – or your banker – is going …

Audition

VERDECCHIA: It's two o'clock on a wintry afternoon, and I have an audition for a TV movie.

A dialect tape plays (see Appendix).

VERDECCHIA prepares for his audition. He puts on a cholo-style shirt and applies dark-brown makeup to his face.

VERDECCHIA: The office has sliding glass doors, hidden light fixtures, and extravagant windows. There are four or five people seated behind a table, including a guy with very expensive sunglasses.

A video camera films VERDECCHIA, direct to monitors.

(*speaking to camera*) Hi, I'm Guillermo Verdecchia. I'm with Noble Talent.

(*speaking to audience*) For those of you who aren't in the business, this is called "slating." Slating is the first thing you do when you audition for a part on a TV show or a movie – you put your face and your name and your agent's name on tape before you read the scene.

(*speaking to camera*) I'm five foot, nine inches. On a good day.

(*speaking to audience*) That's called a little joke. Always good to get the producers and director laughing.

(*speaking to camera*) I'm from Argentina, actually. But I specialize in El Salvadorean refugees, Italian bobsledders, Arab horse thieves, and Uruguayan rugby players who are forced to cannibalize their friends when their plane crashes in the Andes.

(speaking to audience) Actually, I've never played a horse thief or a rugby cannibal, but I have auditioned for them an awful lot.

(speaking to camera) I'm reading for the part of Sharko.

(speaking to audience) An overweight Hispanic in a dirty wife-beater, it says here. I'm perfect for it.

Here we go.

Pop Cops

VERDECCHIA: "A black Camaro in the foreground, the engine throbbing like a hard-on from hell. Cut to close on trunk opening to reveal a deadly assault rifle. We hear SHARKO's voice."

VERDECCHIA slips on a hairnet.

That's me.

VERDECCHIA: *(as SHARKO)* There it is, man. Is a thing of great beauty, no?

Sure, man, I got what you ordered: silencer, bullets. I even got you a little extra, 'cause I like doing business wif you. A shiny new handgun.

Come on, man, it's like brand new. I got it off some old bag who used it to scare away peeping Toms.

Ah, man, you take all this stuff for two grand, and I'll throw in the pistol for a couple of hundred. If you don't like it, you can sell it to some school kids for twice the price.

You already got one, hah? It was a present … I see. A present from who?

From your Uncle Sam. Dat's nice. I diden know you had got an Uncle … (*with dawning horror*) You're a cop?

(*to audience*) Well, that's that. I should've done it differently. I could do the scene again. I can do it differently. I have a bandana I could wear instead of the hairnet.

> Projection (video): The image freezes on
> VERDECCHIA in dark-brown makeup, wearing a
> hairnet.
>
> Projection (text): Ay ay ay ay I am the Frito Bandito
>
> Music: "Cielito Lindo" by Placido Domingo
>
> VERDECCHIA studies his onscreen image and then
> scrubs the makeup off his face.

Santiago Two

VERDECCHIA: I went back to Santiago and looked for some sign of the man who had been shot on the first day of my return. I looked for a stain, a scrape, anything; his shoe perhaps had been left behind. Nothing.

I wondered who he might have been. I remembered the redness of his shirt, the brightness of the sun. It was five o'clock.

A las cinco de la tarde.
Eran las cinco en punto de la tarde.
Un niño trajo la blanca sábana a las cinco de la tarde.[17]

I saw someone die; I watched him die – that's what it looks like – that's where they end up, gunmen, bank robbers, criminals, and those brave revolutionaries and guerrillas you dreamt of and imagined you might be, might have been –

They end up bleeding in the middle of the street, begging for water.

They end up dying alone on the hot pavement in a cheap suit with only one shoe on. People die like that here. Ridiculous, absurd, pathetic deaths.

I came for a sign. I came because I needed to know and now I know.

Projections (images): Photos of the Santiago shooting

¡Que no quiero verla!
Que mi recuerdo se quema.
¡Avisad a los jazmines
con su blancura pequeña!

¡Que no quiero verla!¹⁸

At the hotel they told me he was a bank robber. The papers said the same thing – a bank robber, died almost immediately in a shootout, name: Fernando Ochoa. Case closed. Dead. Gone. Erased.

I told them I was a Canadian writer/journalist/filmmaker. They believed me. They let me look at the files, they let me talk, briefly, to the cops who shot him, and since no one had shown up to claim them, they let me go through his personal effects. There wasn't much: a Bic lighter, with a tiny screw in the bottom so it could be refilled; an empty wallet; a package of cigarettes, with two crumpled Marlboros. There was a letter to someone named Mercedes. It read: "Querida Mercedes: It is bitterly cold tonight in my little room but I can look out the window and see the stars. I imagine that you are looking at them, too. I take comfort in the fact that you and Ines and I share the same sky." There was also a newspaper from August 2, the day I arrived, the day he was shot. The headline claimed that former president Pinochet and the former minister of the interior knew nothing about the bodies that had been found in the Río Mapocho. I asked about his shoe – the one I saw on the road. No one knew anything about a shoe, although they knew he wore size forty-two, just like me.

Decompression

VERDECCHIA: I'm in the bar at Ezeiza, I'm in the bar at Marco Polo, I'm in the bar at Benito Juarez, and I'm decompressing, preparing to surface. I know I'll arrive at Pearson, at Mirabel, at Vancouver International, and I know that nothing will have changed, and that everything will be different. I know that I've left some things behind: a sock in a hotel in Mendoza, a ring in a slum in Rosario, a Zippo lighter in a lobby in Santiago, some toenails in Mauricio's studio in Coyoacán, a combful of hair in the sink in the washroom at Tortoni in Buenos Aires.

These vestiges, these cells, are slowly crawling towards each other. They are crossing oceans and mountains and six-lane expressways. They are calling to each other and arranging to meet in my sleep.

The Therapist

VERDECCHIA: So ... I went to see a therapist. He trained in Vienna but had an office in North York. I didn't tell him that I was afraid my toenails were coming after me in my sleep. I told him, "I have memories of things that never happened to me. I feel nostalgia for things I never knew. I feel connected to things I have no connection with, responsible, involved, implicated in things that happen thousands of miles away."

I answered his questions and showed him the drawings I'd made.

> *Projection (image): VERDECCHIA's combination art naif and art brut drawings*

At about the same time that I started doing what he called "deep therapy work" or what I privately called "reclaiming my inner whale," I began to lose feeling in my extremities. It started as a tingling in the tips of my fingers, and then my hands went numb. Eventually, I lost all feeling in my left arm, and I could hardly lift it.

My therapist told me to see a doctor.

The doctor told me to rest and gave me pills.

Jorge made me go see El Brujo.

I said, "Jorge, what do you mean a brujo? I'm not going to somebody who's gonna sprinkle me with chicken blood and –"

Jorge said, "No, che loco, por favor, dejate de joder, vamos che, tomate un matecito loco y vamos ..."

Who could argue with that? Where is this brujo, Jorge?

"En la frontera."

Where?

"Bloor and Madison."

El Brujo

Music: "Mojotoro" by Dino Saluzzi

Projections (images and video): Footage of the opening sequence from Crucero / Crossroads *overlaid with maps of Bloor and Bathurst area.*[19]

VERDECCHIA: Porque los que recién llegaron me sospechan
porque I speak mejor English que espanish
porque mis padres no me creen
porque hasta mis dreams son subtitled

I went to see El Brujo at his place on Madison, and, you know, I'd been to see a palm reader when I was much younger, so I sort of knew what to expect. And he's this normal guy who actually looks like a very-brown Freddie Prinze, except with much shorter hair. And I told him about my therapist and about the numbness in my body, and El Brujo said, "He tried to steal your soul." And I laughed this kind of honking, sputtering laugh. I thought maybe he was kidding.

El Brujo asked me, "How do you feel?"

And I said, "Okay, aside from the numbness. Well, my stomach is kind of upset."

And he said, "Yes, it is." And I thought, "Oh please, just let me get back to reclaiming my inner whale."

El Brujo said, "You have a very bad Border wound."

I do?

"Yes," he said, "and here en la frontera, of course, Border wounds or afflictions are easily aggravated."

I didn't have the heart to tell him that we were at Bloor and Madison in downtown Toronto.

"Very bad Border wound," he said. "And not all the stray dogs of Santiago, nor all the Lacanians of Recoleta, nor all the rasta hippitecas of el DF can put it back together again …"

El Brujo brought out a bottle, and thinking this would be one way to get my money's worth, I started to drink.

El Brujo said, "I remember the night Bolívar burned with fever and realized there was no way back to the capital; the night he burned his medals and cried, 'Whosoever works for the revolution plows the seas.'"

"You *remember* that do you?" I said. "That was what, 1830 or something?" And I laughed and had another drink. And El Brujo laughed, too, and we had another drink and another drink and another.

El Brujo said, "I remember the Zoot Suit Riots. We were beat up for our pointy shoes and fancy clothes. I still have the scar." And he lifted up his shirt and showed me a gash. It was ugly and ragged and spotted with freshly dried blood. And that's when I first suspected that maybe we weren't at Bloor and Madison. You see, the Zoot Suit Riots were in 1943.[20]

"What do you remember?" he asked.

Not much.

"Try."

I remember the Alamo?

"No, you don't."

No, you're right I don't.

El Brujo said, "Your head aches."

Yes, it does.

"Because your left shoe is too tight. Why don't we burn it?" And maybe because I was drunk already, or maybe because I really thought that burning my shoe would help my headache, we threw it in the bathtub, doused it in lighter fluid, and watched it burn.

"What do you remember now?" he asked.

I remember the French invasion of Mexico; I remember the Pastry War.

I remember the party when Pinochet was finally arrested.

I remember a bar of soap I had when I was little, and it was shaped like a bear or a bunny, and when it got wet, it grew hair, it got all fuzzy.

I remember a little boy in a red snowsuit who ran away whenever anyone spoke to me in English. I remember la machine queso.

I remember a gang of boys who wanted to steal my leather jacket even though we all spoke Spanish; a gang of boys who taught me I could be a long-lost son one minute and a tourist the next.

I remember an audition where I felt I was asked to insult my parents and cousins and people I'd never met, and I remember that I did as I was asked.

I remember practising tai chi outside and being interrupted by a guy who wanted to start a fight, and I remember thinking, "Stupid drunken Mexican." I remember my fear; I taste and smell my fear, my fear of young men who speak Spanish in the darkness of the park, and I know that somewhere in my traitorous heart I can't stand people I claim are my brothers. I don't know who did this to me. I remember feeling sick, I remember howling in the face of my fear.

I remember that I had dreamt I was playing an accordion, playing something improvised that my grandmother recognized after only three notes as a tango from her childhood, playing a tango I had never learned, playing something sad and beautiful not knowing where my fingers were going, playing an accordion, a tango that left me shaking and sweating.

And I remember that I dreamt that dream one night after a party with some Spaniards who kept asking me where I was from and why my Spanish was so funny, and I remember that I remembered that dream the first time one afternoon in Paris while staring at an accordion in a stall at the flea market and then found one hundred francs on the street.

As I passed out, El Brujo said, "The Border is your ..."

Nocturne

Music: "Nocturno a mi Barrio" by Aníbal Troilo

Projection (text): Cuando, cuando me fui?

The Other America

VERDECCHIA: The airport is clean clean clean. And big big big. I'm back in Canada. It's nice. I'm back in Canada ... oh well ...

Why did I come back here?

"This is where I work," I tell myself. "This is where I make the most sense – in this Noah's ark of a nation."

I reach into my pocket, expecting to find a book of matches and my last package of Particulares, but instead I find a Bic lighter with a tiny screw in the bottom so it can be refilled and a package of Marlboros with two crumpled cigarettes in it. And written on the package is a note, a quotation I hadn't noticed before. It says, "No estoy en el crucero: elegir es equivocarse."[21]

> Projection (text): I am not at the crossroads;
> to choose is to go wrong. – Octavio Paz

And then I remember. I remember what El Brujo said. He said, "The Border is your Home."

I'm not in Canada; I'm not in Argentina.

I'm on the Border.

I am Home.

Mais zooot alors, je comprends maintenant, mais oui, merde! Je suis Argentin-Canadien! I am a post-Porteño neo-Latino Canadian! I am the Pan-American Highway!

Latin Invasion

WIDELOAD: It's okay, mang. Everybody relax. I'm back. Ya, I been lying low in dis act but let me tell you, I'm here to stay.

And it's quiz time. Please cast your memories way back and tell me who remembers José Jiménez?

Aha.

Who remembers de Frito Bandito? Who remembers Cheech and Chong?

Who remembers de U.S. invasion of Panama? Who remembers the Harper government and the Obama administration recently endorsing a coup in Honduras?

Dat's okay; dat was a trick question.[22]

Who remembers de ad dat McDonald's had for deir fajitas not too long ago featuring a guy called Pedro or Juan, and he says dat he's up here to get some McFajitas because (*reciting with supreme nasality*) "dese are de most gueno fajitas I eber ate." What de fuck ees dat?

Can you imagine an ad dat went like: "Hey, Sambo, what are you doing here?"

"Well, mistah, I come up here to get some o' yo' pow'ful good McGrits. Mmmmm-mmm. Wif a watahmelon slice fo' deesert. Yassee."

I mean, we would be shocked, offended. But that was a long time ago. Or was it? I got this in the mail just the other day.

Projection (image): Quesada's "Real Mexican" ad

So, what is it with you people? Who do you think you are? Who do you think we are?

Yes, I am calling you "you" – I am generalizing, I am reducing you all to de lowest common denominator, I am painting you all with the same brush. Is it starting to bug you yet?

Of course, it is possible dat it doesn't really matter what I say. Because it's all been kind of funny dis evening.

Dat has been my mistake. I have wanted you to like me so I've been a funny guy.

    Silence.

Esto, en serio ahora –

Señoras y señores, globalization, migration, we are redrawing the map of America. Dis is a big deal and very complicated. And I wish to remind you, at this crucial juncture in our shared geographies, dat under dose funny voices and under dose funny images and under all the talk we hear of money and markets, there are living, breathing, dreaming men, women, and children.

I want to ask you please to throw out the metaphor of Latin America as North America's backyard, because your backyard is now a Border, and the metaphor is now made flesh. Mira, I am in your backyard. I live next door, I live upstairs, I live across de street. It's me, your neighbour, your dance partner.

    Projection (text): Towards un futuro post-Columbian

Consider

WIDELOAD & VERDECCHIA: (*variously*) Consider those come from the plains, del litoral, from the steppes, from the desert, from the savannah, from the Fens, from the sertão, from the rainforest, from the sierras, from the hills and high places.

Consider those come from the many corners of the globe to Fort McMurray, to Montreal, to St. John's to build, to teach, to navigate ships, to weave, to stay, to remember, to dream.

Consider those here first. Consider those I have not considered. Consider your parents, consider your grandparents.

Consider the country. Consider the continent. Consider the Border.

Going Forward

VERDECCHIA: I am learning to live the Border. I have called off the Border patrol. I am a hyphenated person, but I am not falling apart; I am putting together. I am building a house on the Border that, I hope, others, perhaps my children, maybe yours, will come to live in.

And you? Did you change your name somewhere along the way? Does a part of you live hundreds or thousands of kilometres away? Do you have two countries, two memories?

Will you call off the Border patrol?

Ladies and gentlemen, please reset your watches. It is now almost ten o'clock on a (Friday) night – we still have time. We can go forward. Towards the centre, towards the Border.

WIDELOAD: And let the dancing begin!

Music: "African Battle" by Brownout

Appendix Dialect Tape

Tape to be played while VERDECCHIA prepares for his audition.

(*unaccented*) Let us now review the keys to the Spanish accent: forward "tone focus."

(*accented*) Lift the tongue tip toward the aveolar ridge to help focus the resonance. The vibrations will seem to spill forward into the nasal cavity.

(*unaccented*) Pronunciation changes.

(*accented*) Especially important is the trilled or tapped *R*, as in rrrose, arrrive, and fearrrrrrrrrrrrrrrrrrrrrrrrrrrrrrrrrrrrrrrrrrr.

(*unaccented*) Don't forget your consonant subsitutions such as ...

(*accented*) CHesterday.

(*unaccented*) And extra aspiration:

(*accented*) HHHHenry HHHHarrison is frrrrrrom ManHHHHattan.

(*unaccented*) Be careful to create the resonance properly, and not to overdo the lilt ...

(*accented*) ... unless it's for comedic effects.

(*unaccented*) Let's practise ...

Notes

1   Carlos Fuentes's 1984 Massey Lectures, published as *Latin America: At War with the Past* (Montreal: CBC Enterprises, 1985) elegantly explore, in greater detail, the divisions expressed by the Mexico-U.S. border. See also his essay "How I Started to Write," in *Myself with Others* (New York: Farrar, Straus, and Giroux, 1990). Although Fuentes focuses almost exclusively on the United States, his analysis and insight provide a useful perspective and reference point for Canadians. Likewise, Octavio Paz, *The Labyrinth of Solitude: Life and Thought in Mexico* (New York: Grove Press, 1961), seemed to me, when I first wrote this play, useful to us in Canada as we grappled with borders and our relationship with the United States.

2   William Langewiesche, "The Border," *Atlantic* vol. 269, no. 5 (May 1992): 53–92. This excellent article deals specifically with the Mexico-U.S. border, border crossings, border patrols, drug trafficking, and economics.

3   To say nothing of the Minutemen and the various splinter groups of self-appointed border vigilantes.

4   Approximately forty thousand people annually take *favela* tours in Brazil. The numbers for similar kinds of tourism are much higher in India and South Africa. See, for a start, Amy Stillman, "Rio Seeks to Boost Favela Tourism," BBC News, November 9, 2010, http://www.bbc.co.uk/news /world-latin-america-11568243; and Manfred Rolfes, "Poverty Tourism: Theoretical Reflections and Empirical Findings Regarding an Extraordinary Form of Tourism" in *GeoJournal* (December 2010): 421–42.

5   In the 1993 draft, the explanation was more fulsome: "Dere is a world of difference between de right wing Cubans living in Miami and exiled Salvadorean leftists living in Canada, between Mexican speakers of Nahuatl and Brazilian speakers of Portuguese, between a Tico and a Nuyorican (dat's a Puerto Rican who lives in New York), and den dere's de Uruguayans. I mean, dey're practically European."

6   See Luis Valdez, *Zoot Suit* (San Juan Bautista, CA: Teatro Campesino, 2002).

7   Alwyn Barr, *Texans in Revolt: The Battle for San Antonio, 1835* (Austin: University of Texas Press, 1990).

8   Macias, Maria, and Fatima Torres, "Mennonite Colonies in Mexico Accept Change Slowly," *Borderlands* 19 (2000–01): 13, http://dnn.epcc.edu/nwlibrary/borderlands.

9   For further discussion about the shift from production to consumption, and especially the consumption of images, see Jean Baudrillard, and, oh, Fredric Jameson, for starters.

10 In the first edition, Wideload was pursuing Chicano studies: "I practically have a doctorate in Chicano estudies. Dat's right – Chicano estudies ... Well not exactly a doctorate – more like an MA or most of an MA – 'cause I got my credits all screwed up and I diden finish – my professors said I was ungovernable. I lacked discipline. You know, instead of, like, doing a paper on de historical roots of the oppression of La Raza, I organized an all-night salsa dance party extravaganza. I also organized de month long *Chico and de Man* memorial symposium, which I dedicated to my cousing Esperanza, back home."

11 The first edition used Roberto Goyeneche's version of "Vuelvo Al Sur," which featured Ástor Piazzolla.

12 Lynn Snowden, "Latin Lovers and Mambo Kings: Playing Truth or Dare with Antonio Banderas," *Elle*, November 1991.

13 See Bernardo Verbitsky's novel *Villa Miseria también es América* (Buenos Aires: Paidos, 1967) and Antonio Berni's *Juanito Laguna* paintings.

14 This section might change somewhat depending on the composition of the audience. Wideload might instead say, "Nice mix of people tonight. 'Cause usually is almost blinding when the lights come up, dere are so many white people ... And how weird dey congregate so in theatres," etc.

15 Gonzalo Fernández de Oviedo y Valdés et al., *General and Natural History of the Indies, Islands, and Mainlands of the Ocean* (Berkeley, 1941). See also *The Four Voyages of Christopher Columbus*, ed. J.M. Cohen (London: Cresset Library, 1988), 27. Earlier productions quoted Carlos Fuentes, *Latin America at War with the Past*: "Every North American, before this century is over, will find that he or she has a personal frontier with Latin America.

    This is a living frontier, which can be nourished by information, but above all, by knowledge, by understanding, by the pursuit of enlightened self-interest on both parts.

    Or it can be starved by suspicion, ghost stories, arrogance, scorn, and violence."

16 These movies make no mention of the enormous amounts of money made in militarizing and "securing" the border in the name of controlling the flow of drugs. For more on drug politics, see Peter Dale Scott and John Marshall, *Cocaine Politics: Drugs, Armies, and the CIA in Central America* (Berkeley:

University of California Press, 1991); Ed Vulliamy, "How a Big U.S. Bank Laundered Billions from Mexico's Murderous Drug Gangs," *Observer*, Sunday, April 3, 2011, http://www.guardian.co.uk/world/2011/apr/03/us-bank-mexico-drug-gangs; Charles Bowden and Julian Cardona, *Murder City: Ciudad Juarez and the Global Economy's New Killing Fields* (New York: Nation Books, 2010); and Malcolm Beith, *The Last Narco: Hunting El Chapo, the World's Most Wanted Drug Lord* (London: Penguin, 2010). Finally, have a look at the U.S. General Accounting Office's June 1999 report to Congressional Requesters, "Narcotics Threat from Colombia Continues to Grow," for an admission from the heart of the U.S. administration that the so-called War on Drugs is a failure in terms of controlling the flow of drugs into the United States.

17 Federico Garíca Lorca, "La cogida y la muerte," in *Poema del cante jondo / Llanto por Ignacio Sánchez Mejías* (Buenos Aires: Editorial Losada, 1948), 145.

18 Federico García Lorca, "Llanto por Ignacio Sanchez Mejias," in *The Selected Poems of Federico García Lorca* (New York: New Directions, 2005), 138–40.

19 Earlier productions quoted *Border Brujo*, Guillermo Gómez-Peña: "The West is no longer west. The old binary models have been replaced by a border dialectic of ongoing flux. We now inhabit a social universe in constant motion, a moving cartography with a floating culture and a fluctuating sense of self."

20 The L.A. Zoot Suit Riots occurred in 1943. But there were also Zoot Suit "disturbances" in Montreal in 1944. See Serge Marc Durflinger, "The Montreal and Verdun Zoot-Suit Disturbances of June 1944," on the Canadian Museum of Civilization website: www.civilization.ca.

21 Octavio Paz, "A La Mitad de Esta Frase," in *The Collected Poems of Octavio Paz, 1957–1987*, ed. Eliot Weinberger (New York: New Directions, 1991), 372.

22 Although the Organization of American States, the United Nations, and governments across Latin America condemned the coup that deposed the elected Honduran president, Manuel Zelaya, Canada and the United States were equivocal in their responses. Canada repeatedly called for "both sides" to show restraint in the aftermath of the coup, as if the deposed president was somehow as culpable as the golpistas for the tense situation. When elections were held to lend an air of legitimacy to the coup and its leaders, Peter Kent, MP for Thornhill, Ontario, and minister of state of foreign affairs (Americas) might have said, "Canada does not recognize this government," or "Canada rejects the results of this fraudulent election held under a cloud of violence and intimidation and stands with all Hondurans who respect and practise democracy." Instead he announced, "As Hondurans begin this new

59

chapter in their history, Canada stands ready to assist with the challenges that lie ahead." Thereby, the government put the unpleasantness behind them, and got back to the business of business.

For more about the coup, listen to the interviews on *The Current* at http://www.cbc.ca/thecurrent/2009/07/july-29-2009.html and see also, among many other articles, Rory Carroll, "Honduras Coup: Troops Deployed to Oversee Election," *Guardian*, November 27, 2009, http://www.guardian.co.uk/world/2009/nov/27/honduras-election-troops-deployed-zelaya; and Todd Gordon and Jeffrey Weber, "Canada and the Honduran Coup," *Bulletin of Latin American Research* 30 (2011): 328–43.

Acknowledgements

I'd like to acknowledge Peter Hinton, Candace Burley, Iris Turcott, and Canadian Stage; Janette and Doug Pirie, who lodged me back then; Urjo Kareda and the Tarragon Theatre; the Ontario Arts Council, the Canada Council for the Arts; Damon D'Oliviera; Tamsin Kelsey, who put up with me while I wrote *Fronteras* and continues to put up with me today; Jim Warren, whose gentle and intelligent dramaturgy refined the original script and this revision, and whose faith in the play was crucial both then and now. Finally, I want to thank those generous audience members who came to listen and stayed to share their Border stories.

GUILLERMO VERDECCHIA is a writer of drama, fiction, and film, and a director, dramaturge, actor, and translator whose work has been seen and heard on stages, screens, and radios across Canada and around the globe. He is the author, or co-author, of, among other works, *Citizen Suárez*; *Another Country*; *Insomnia* and *The Noam Chomsky Lectures* (with Daniel Brooks); *Fronteras Americanas*; *The Terrible But Incomplete Journals of John D.*; *bloom*; *A Line in the Sand* (with Marcus Youssef); and the controversial *Adventures of Ali & Ali and the aXes of Evil* (with Camyar Chai and Marcus Youssef). Verdecchia is a recipient of the Governor General's Award for Drama, a four-time winner of the Chalmers Canadian Play Award, a recipient of Dora and Jessie Awards, and sundry film festival awards for his 1994 film *Crucero / Crossroads*, based on *Fronteras Americanas* and made with Ramiro Puerta.